WHO IS
the
HOLY SPIRIT?

The Crucial Questions Series
By R. C. Sproul

CRUCIAL
QUESTIONS
No. | 13

WHO IS
the
HOLY SPIRIT?

R.C. SPROUL

ℝ *Reformation Trust*   A DIVISION OF LIGONIER MINISTRIES, ORLANDO, FL

Who Is the Holy Spirit?

© 2012 by R. C. Sproul

Published by Reformation Trust Publishing
a division of Ligonier Ministries
421 Ligonier Court, Sanford, FL 32771
Ligonier.org   ReformationTrust.com

Printed in North Mankato, MN
Corporate Graphics
November 2012
First edition

Cover design: Gearbox Studios
Interior design and typeset: Katherine Lloyd, The DESK

Library of Congress Cataloging-in-Publication Data

Sproul, R. C. (Robert Charles), 1939-
  Who is the Holy Spirit? / R. C. Sproul.
    p. cm. -- (The crucial questions series ; no. 13)
  ISBN 978-1-56769-299-0
1. Holy Spirit. I. Title.
  BT121.3.S67 2012
  231'.3--dc23

                                      2012027502

Contents

Preface

When I became a Christian in September of 1957, I found myself in a serious quandary. I was engaged to be married, but when I told my fiancée about my conversion, she thought I had lost my mind. That was upsetting enough, but I was also learning that I should not marry a nonbeliever, and so I began to wonder whether I would be able to marry the woman I loved. Several months passed with no resolution of this dilemma.

Finally, spring break approached. My fiancée was planning to go home to Pittsburgh from the college where she was studying, and I persuaded her to stop at my college, attend a campus Bible study with me, and then spend the night in the girls' dorm. I cannot remember anything for which I spent more time praying. I spent virtually the whole day before she arrived on my knees, praying that God would work in her life. I came to the conclusion that if she did not soon become a Christian, I would have to break the engagement, as much as I did not want to do so.

We went to the Bible study that night and she sat through the whole thing without saying a word. Afterward, I took her to the girls' dorm, and she was still very quiet. However, the next morning, when I went to meet her, she came out as if she were walking on air. She told me that she had had a hard time sleeping because something had happened to her the night before. She kept waking up in the night, pinching herself, and asking, "Do I still have it?" Each time she told herself, "Yes, I still have it," and went back to sleep. She had been converted to Christ through the study of the Scriptures the night before.

One of my clearest memories of that wonderful morning is of the moment when we were getting into my car. As she was telling me about her experience, she looked at me with great excitement and said, "Now I know who the Holy Spirit is." Of course, she had attended church for years. She had heard the Holy Spirit mentioned. She had heard the benediction pronounced in the name of the Father, the Son, and the Holy Spirit. But now, for the first time, she had a sense of who the Spirit really is.

That statement of my fiancée, who is now my wife, was very significant. Notice that she said, "Now I know *who* the Holy Spirit is," not, "Now I know *what* the Holy Spirit is." In her conversion, she made a transition from understanding Christianity in an abstract sense to understanding it as a personal relationship with God. And one of the first truths she grasped was that the Holy Spirit is a person, not a thing.

It is exceedingly important that Christians know who the Holy Spirit is and understand something of the vital role He plays in their lives. That is why I have written this booklet. Of course, the biblical teaching on the Holy Spirit is far too extensive to be covered adequately in a volume of this size. My purpose in this booklet is to simply provide the most basic of answers to the question of who the Spirit is and then to touch briefly on some of the important roles

He plays in the lives of believers. For a fuller treatment, I encourage you to see my book *The Mystery of the Holy Spirit*.

I pray this short treatise on the Spirit will draw you into a deeper relationship with the God you love and serve, Father, Son, and Holy Spirit.

Chapter One

THE THIRD PERSON

As Christians, we embrace a historic formula about God's being. We say, "God is One in essence and three in person." In other words, God is triune; He is a Trinity. This means there are three persons within the Godhead. These persons are understood in theology as distinct characters. The differences among the three, the Father, Son, and Holy Spirit, are real differences but not essential differences. In other words, there is only one essence to the Godhead, not three. In our experience as human beings, each person we meet is a separate being. One person means one being, and vice versa. But in the Godhead, there is one being with three persons. We must maintain this distinction lest we slip into a form of polytheism, seeing the three persons of the Godhead as three beings who are three separate gods.

None of us can plumb the depths of the Trinity comprehensively, but we can take some small steps to understand it better. The words *existence* and *subsistence* can help us here.

EXISTENCE AND SUBSISTENCE

One of the games I used to play with my seminary students was to ask them, "Does God exist?" They would say, "Of course God exists." I would then say, "No, God does not exist," and it was always fun to see the looks of horror that would appear on their faces as they began to wonder whether their professor had abandoned Christianity and given up his faith. But I quickly had mercy on them and explained that I was playing a little philosophy game by asserting that God does not exist.

The word *exist* comes from the Latin *existare*, which means "to stand out of." So the word *exist* literally means "to stand out." That does not necessarily mean that if you exist you are outstanding at what you do. The obvious question is, of what does an existing being stand out?

The idea of existence has its roots in ancient philosophy, when the philosophers were very concerned with the question of being. We also are concerned with this question; in fact, when we make a distinction between God and ourselves, we identify Him as the Supreme Being and ourselves as human beings. However, that distinction is a bit misleading. Both descriptions use the word *being*, so we look to the adjectival qualifiers to find the difference between God and ourselves: He is supreme and we are human. In reality, the big difference between God and man is being itself. God is pure being, a being who has His life in and of Himself eternally. A human being is a creature, a being whose very existence from moment to moment depends on the power of the Supreme Being. God's being is not dependent on anything or derived from anything. He has the power to be in and of Himself.

When the old philosophers talked about existence, using the Latin word meaning "to stand out of," they were saying that to exist means to stand out of being. What does that mean? Imagine two circles that do not overlap. The first circle is "being" and the second is "non-being," which is a fancy term for "nothing." Now imagine a stick figure between the two circles with its arms outstretched. One arm is reaching into the circle labeled "being" and the other is reaching into the circle labeled "non-being." This is a picture of humanity. We participate in being, but at the same time we are always just one step away from annihilation. The only way we can continue is to maintain our connection to the circle labeled "being," for that circle represents the One in whom, as the Apostle Paul said, "we live and move and have our being" (Acts 17:28)—that is, God. But even while we participate in that being and are sustained by that being, we are one step removed from non-being.

Our imaginary stick figure is a picture of what the philosophers had in mind when they talked about standing out of being. We might say that humans are in a state of "becoming." We undergo change. What we are today is different from what we were yesterday and from what we will be tomorrow, if only in the fact that we age twenty-four hours in the passage from one day to the next. It is this facet of humanness, change, that defines existence. Change, generation, decay, growth, and aging are all characteristics of our lives. God, however, is eternally constant. He is the same yesterday, today, and forever.

In short, when the philosophers spoke of existence, they were defining what it means to be a creature. So, when I played my little game with my seminary students, when I asserted that God does not exist, I did not mean that there is no God. I simply meant that God is not a creature. He is not bound to space and time, subject to change, generation, and decay. He is always and eternally what He is. He is the "I AM."

When we talk about the persons of the Godhead, we typically do not use the word *existence*, but we do use the word *subsistence*. What is the difference between these words? We typically use the word *subsistence* in our normal vocabulary when we talk about someone living in poverty. We talk about a subsistence income, which is a meager wage, or a subsistence diet, which provides only the basic nutrients. Note, however, that this word includes the prefix *sub-*, which means "under." So, subsistence is existence that is under something else. This idea is implied in the concept of the Trinity. God is one being with three subsistences, with three distinct persons. They subsist within the being of God.

THE SPIRIT'S PERSONAL NATURE

The fact that the Holy Spirit is a person is seen in a multitude of ways in Scripture. One of the primary evidences is that the Bible repeatedly and consistently uses personal pronouns to refer to Him. He is called "He," "Him," and so on, not "it." Also, He does things that we associate with personality. He teaches, He inspires, He guides, He leads, He grieves, He convicts us of sin, and more. Impersonal objects do not behave in this manner. Only a person can do these things.

But the Holy Spirit is seen in Scripture not merely as personal but also as fully divine. We see this in a curious story from the book of Acts:

> But a man named Ananias, with his wife Sapphira, sold a piece of property, and with his wife's knowledge he kept back for himself some of the proceeds and brought only a part of it and laid it at the apostles' feet. But Peter said, "Ananias, why has Satan filled your heart to lie to the Holy Spirit and to keep back for yourself part of the proceeds of the land? While it remained unsold, did it not remain your

own? And after it was sold, was it not at your disposal? Why is it that you have contrived this deed in your heart? You have not lied to man but to God." (5:1–4)

The sin of Ananias and Sapphira was that they pretended that their donation to the church was greater than it was. They lied about the nature of the gift they were making to God. Peter, I think, was more concerned about the state of their souls than about the amount of money they were contributing. Notice, however, the words of Peter's rebuke to Ananias and Sapphira. He began by asking, "Ananias, why has Satan filled your heart to lie to the Holy Spirit?" But he concluded by saying, "You have not lied to man but to God." So, the lie that Ananias told to the Holy Spirit was actually told to God. The clear implication is that the Holy Spirit is God.

ATTRIBUTES AND WORKS OF GOD

Furthermore, the New Testament often describes the Holy Spirit as having attributes that are clearly divine. For instance, the Holy Spirit is eternal (Heb. 9:14) and omniscient

(1 Cor. 2:10–11). These are both attributes of God. Moreover, they are incommunicable attributes, attributes of God that cannot be shared by man.

We see in Scripture that the Spirit shares in the Trinitarian works of creation and redemption. Genesis 1 shows that the Father commanded the world to come into being. The New Testament tells us that the agent through whom the Father brought the universe into being was the *Logos,* the second person of the Trinity, our Lord Jesus Christ: "All things were made through him, and without him was not any thing made that was made" (John 1:3). However, the Spirit also was involved in creation: "The Spirit of God was hovering over the face of the waters" (Gen. 1:2). Out of this energizing work of the Spirit, life was brought forth.

Most importantly, redemption is a Trinitarian work. The Father sent the Son into the world (1 John 4:14). The Son performed all the work that was necessary for our salvation—living a life of perfect obedience and dying to make a perfect satisfaction (Phil. 3:9; 1 Cor. 15:3). But none of these things avail for our benefit until they are applied to us personally. Therefore, the Father and the Son send the Holy Spirit into the world to apply salvation to us (John 15:26; Gal. 4:6). The role of the Holy Spirit chiefly and principally in the New Testament is to apply the work of Christ to believers.

Do you know who the Holy Spirit is? Do you understand the Holy Spirit in terms of a personal relationship? Or does the Spirit remain for you a vague, misty, abstract concept or an illusive, amorphous force? Forces in and of themselves are impersonal. But the Holy Spirit is not simply an abstract force. He is a person who empowers the people of God for the Christian life. In the next few brief chapters, we will consider some of the ways He carries out that mission.

Chapter Two

THE LIFE GIVER

During the 1976 campaign for the United States presidency, Jimmy Carter spoke of having been "born again." Around that same time, Charles Colson, who had been an adviser to President Nixon, released a book recounting his conversion to Christ. It was titled simply *Born Again*. Suddenly, a term that had been common only among evangelical Christians was catapulted to national prominence.

Since then, the term "born again" has been adopted for all kinds of uses that have nothing to do with the kind of spiritual conversion Carter and Colson had in mind. For instance, an athlete who experiences a comeback in his career might speak of being "born again" with respect to his skills. There is a sense in which the true meaning of this important term has become obscured by its frequent use and misuse.

The idea of being born again, of experiencing a spiritual rebirth, comes directly from the teaching of Jesus. We find that teaching in the third chapter of John's Gospel, where John records an encounter between Jesus and a Jewish leader named Nicodemus.

John writes: "Now there was a man of the Pharisees named Nicodemus, a ruler of the Jews. This man came to Jesus by night and said to him, 'Rabbi, we know that you are a teacher come from God, for no one can do these signs that you do unless God is with him'" (vv. 1–2). Nicodemus came to Jesus at night, apparently because he did not want to be seen with Him, but he came with flattery, complimenting Jesus as "a teacher come from God." However, Jesus cut him short and said, "Truly, truly, I say to you, unless one is born again he cannot see the kingdom of God" (v. 3). Jesus said that rebirth is a necessary condition for entering the kingdom of God. It is the *sine qua non*. If you are not regenerate, you cannot enter the kingdom of God.

Nicodemus did not understand Him; he interpreted Jesus' words in a crass, physical way. He asked: "How can a man be born when he is old? Can he enter a second time into his mother's womb and be born?" (v. 4). Jesus answered him a second time and said, "Truly, truly, I say to you, unless one is born of water and the Spirit, he cannot enter the kingdom of God" (v. 5). So, the idea of being born again or experiencing rebirth was not invented by Jimmy Carter, Chuck Colson, or evangelical Christians in general. It is found in the teaching of Christ Himself. This teaching is extremely important, because in it, Jesus mentions a necessary condition for entering the kingdom of God.

It distresses me somewhat to hear a person say, "I am a born-again Christian." What's wrong with such a statement? Well, what other kind of Christian is there? If rebirth is absolutely essential in order to get into the kingdom of God, as Jesus said it is, there cannot be such a thing as a non-born-again Christian. To say "born-again Christian" is like saying "Christian Christian." It's a redundancy, a kind of theological stuttering.

On the other hand, is it possible to be a "born-again non-Christian"? I have heard people say, "I'm a born-again

Muslim" or "I'm a born-again Buddhist." I want to tell them that if they are born again in the New Testament sense, they no longer are Muslims or Buddhists. The only people who are born again are Christians.

FROM SPIRITUAL DEATH TO LIFE

It is very important that we have an accurate understanding of the work of the Holy Spirit in spiritual rebirth. One of the best places to gain such an understanding is in the second chapter of the Apostle Paul's letter to the Ephesians. We read there:

> And you were dead in the trespasses and sins in which you once walked, following the course of this world, following the prince of the power of the air, the spirit that is now at work in the sons of disobedience—among whom we all once lived in the passions of our flesh, carrying out the desires of the body and the mind, and were by nature children of wrath, like the rest of mankind. But God, being rich in mercy, because of the great love with which he loved us, even when we were dead in our trespasses,

made us alive together with Christ— by grace you have been saved—and raised us up with him and seated us with him in the heavenly places in Christ Jesus. (vv. 1–6)

The language and imagery the Apostle uses in this text has to do with life and death. He declares that Christians have been "made alive." But if they are now alive, what were they previously? They were "dead in trespasses and sins." So, Paul is talking about some kind or resurrection, a transformation of people who are dead to new life.

We need to understand what kind of death is in view here. Paul is not talking about physical resurrection because he is not talking about physical death. The people who have been made alive by the Holy Spirit were living, breathing biological specimens before that experience. Before I became a Christian, my heart was beating, my lungs were filling and emptying, and my brain was active (although my teachers wondered at times). But I was spiritually dead. I was dead to the things of God because I existed solely and completely in what Jesus and the Apostles call "the flesh."

In His conversation with Nicodemus, after He explained that no one can enter the kingdom of God unless he is born of water and the Spirit, Jesus went on to say: "That which is born of the flesh is flesh, and that which is born of the Spirit is spirit. Do not marvel that I said to you, 'You must be born again.' The wind blows where it wishes, and you hear its sound, but you do not know where it comes from or where it goes. So it is with everyone who is born of the Spirit" (John 3:6–8).

Here Jesus distinguished between the power of the Holy Spirit and the power of human flesh. He said, "That which is born of the flesh is flesh." He was speaking of people, and He was not simply saying that human beings are born with physical bodies, but that they are born fallen. This means they do not have spiritual life. Instead, they are born spiritually dead.

There may be nothing in all of sacred Scripture that is more repugnant to modern man than this assertion that every human being is born into a state of spiritual death. This idea is repugnant even to the broad Christian community. Most professing Christians acknowledge that there is some defect in the human race, that we are all sinners and none of us is perfect. But not one Christian in a hundred really believes that every human being is already spiritually dead when he or she comes into the world. Even Billy

Graham used to talk about the natural man being mortally sick, to the extent that he is ninety-nine percent dead, but he would not go to one hundred percent. So pervasive is the rejection of this idea that some of the leading spokesmen for Christianity are willing to contradict it. They do not embrace the idea of total spiritual death.

Yet, that is clearly what Paul is saying. We are dead on arrival spiritually—not just weak, ailing, critically ill, or comatose. There is no spiritual heartbeat, no spiritual breathing, no spiritual brain-wave activity. We are spiritually stillborn, and so we remain—unless God the Holy Spirit makes us alive.

FOLLOWING A COURSE AND A PRINCE

Paul tells the Ephesians, "You were dead in the trespasses and sins in which you once walked, following the course of this world, following the prince of the power of the air" (2:1). He is addressing Christians, but all Christians at some point in their lives are non-Christians, and all non-Christians manifest a pattern of behavior. Paul says that those who are spiritually dead follow a course and a prince.

In Romans 3, Paul writes: "None is righteous, no,

not one; no one understands; no one seeks for God. All have turned aside; together they have become worthless; no one does good, not even one" (vv. 10b–12). He says everyone has "turned aside," has gone out of the way. If by nature we do not seek God, is it any surprise that we should depart from the way to God? It is fascinating to me that in the New Testament, followers of Christ did not refer to themselves as "Christians." They were first called Christians at Antioch (Acts 11:26), but it is believed that the term was created by non-Christians to hurl derision on them. The word or the phrase that Christians used to describe themselves initially was people of "the Way" (Acts 19:9, 23), because they had heard Christ speak about two ways, a narrow way and a broad way (Matt. 7:13–14). The vast majority of people are moving down the wrong road. In fact, we all start on this road, for the broad way is the course of the world. Paul says, "This is the way we all lived at one time" (see Eph. 2:3). To be spiritually dead is to be worldly. It is to buy into and follow slavishly the values and customs of the secular culture.

Not only do the spiritually dead follow the course of this world, they follow "the prince of the power of the air"

(v. 2). Is there any question about who Paul has in mind here? This is his title for Satan, "the spirit that is now at work in the sons of disobedience" (v. 2). All those who are spiritually dead follow the desires of Satan in rejecting God and His righteous requirements.

This, then, is our natural state. This is a picture of what theology calls original sin, that state of mortal corruption, of spiritual death, into which we all are born.

A WORK OF RE-CREATION

It is the ministry and work of the Holy Spirit to come to people who are spiritually dead, who are walking according to the course of this world and according to the prince of the power of the air, fulfilling the lusts of their flesh and of their minds, and to re-create them as He regenerates them. "To regenerate" means "to generate anew." By means of regeneration, the Spirit gives life to people who have no spiritual life.

Regeneration is a work that the Holy Spirit does immediately upon the souls of people. When I say "immediately," I do not mean "quickly" but "without any intervening medium." He does not give a person a dose of medicine; instead, the Spirit directly brings spiritual life out of spiritual death. We see this immediate working expressed in the words the angel Gabriel spoke to Mary: "The Holy Spirit will come upon you, and the power of the Most High will overshadow you" (Luke 1:35). In that situation, Jesus' life was generated immediately and directly, not through the normal reproductive processes.

In this sense, we see a kind of recapitulation in redemption of the power the Holy Spirit manifested in creation. The same God who created the world redeems the world. The work of creation was Trinitarian just as the work of redemption is Trinitarian. We see this clearly in Genesis 1, where we read: "In the beginning, God created the heavens and the earth. The earth was without form and void, and darkness was over the face of the deep" (vv. 1–2a). These are the first sentences of sacred Scripture. Immediately after these verses, we read a brief description of God's activity in the midst of this darkness, emptiness, and formlessness: "And the Spirit of God was hovering over the face of the waters" (v. 2b). The Holy Spirit is pictured in the New Testament as a dove; here He is possibly depicted as a mother bird hovering over her chicks to protect them. Jesus expressed something of this concept when He lamented over the city of Jerusalem and said: "O Jerusalem, Jerusalem, the city that kills the prophets and stones those who are sent to it! How often would I have gathered your children together as a hen gathers her brood under her wings, and you were not willing!" (Luke 13:34). The Spirit hovered over the creation to guide and protect it, and so He does in the work of regeneration.

Scripture makes clear that one of the things that God and God alone can do is to bring life out of death and something out of nothing. The next thing that happened in creation was God's creation of light: "And God said, 'Let there be light,' and there was light" (Gen. 1:3). God did not need to turn a switch or rub two sticks together to create a spark to create the light. His sovereign command formed the light. In the same way, His divine power brings life where there is no life.

Jesus stood at the tomb of Lazarus, who had been dead for four days, and shouted in a loud voice, "Lazarus, come out" (John 11:43). When Jesus spoke those words, Lazarus' heart instantly began to beat and pump blood. Brain activity resumed. Life returned to the body, and he came forth from the tomb. That is exactly what happens to us in our rebirth. The same Spirit who brought life out of the abyss and who brought Lazarus back from the grave raises us from spiritual death by causing us to be born a second time.

Chapter Three

THE ADVOCATE

In the nineteenth century, two philosophers in Europe made an enormous impact on their culture and on subsequent history. Both of them were very concerned about the corruption of Western civilization. Both of them described nineteenth-century Europe as decadent. But the two of them saw very different reasons for that decadence and proposed very different solutions.

One of them was Søren Kierkegaard (1813–55), a Danish philosopher. He complained that the reason for the decadence of civilization in his age was a failure to apply

Christianity in a vital way to daily life. He believed that Christianity had largely become a dead orthodoxy that was dispassionate and removed from day-to-day matters. As he put it, his age was "paltry." Therefore, he cried out for the return of passion to the Christian life. When he became discouraged about this, he liked to turn to the pages of the Old Testament, for there he found people who seemed more real. They were saints and sinners, and there was nothing phony, fake, or artificial about them. God really worked in their lives, and they, in turn, had a passion for Him.

Another professor once asked me, "How do you assess the strength of the church today?" I replied that it was becoming increasingly clear to me that many people in the church have a vibrant faith, believe the cardinal doctrines of Scripture, and so forth, but few of them see the Christian faith as a mission, as a profound concern in their lives. That was what Kierkegaard longed to see.

The other philosopher who decried the death of civilization was Friedrich Nietzsche (1844–1900), a German. However, Nietzsche believed the biggest problem with Western civilization was the baleful influence of Christianity. He was convinced that the ethic of Christianity, with its virtues of meekness and kindness, had emasculated the human race. He felt that Christianity denied and undercut the most basic human passion of all—the will to power. Life, Nietzsche said, is a power struggle. All of us are engaged in a competitive enterprise, seeking dominance over others.

So, Nietzsche called for a new civilization that would be brought in by a new kind of human being, a new kind of existential hero, which he called the *übermench*, the "superman." He described the superman as one who would build his home on the slopes of the volcano Mount Vesuvius. Thus, he would build his home in a place where it might be destroyed at any moment, should the volcano erupt. Likewise, he would sail his ship into uncharted seas. He might encounter sea monsters or tempests that would capsize his ship and kill him, but that would be no hindrance to the superman.

According to Nietzsche's concept, the superman is chiefly a conqueror and his chief virtue is courage, for Nietzsche believed that courage was the main thing lacking in nineteenth-century culture. But when Nietzsche spoke about courage, he gave it a strange spin. He called for "dialectical courage." In philosophy, the word *dialectical* has to do with a state of contradiction, wherein something stands as an antithesis to something else. These things can never be resolved. What, then, is dialectical courage? Nietzsche came to the conclusion that life ultimately is nihilistic or meaningless. He believed God is dead, and since there is no God, there is no such thing as absolute goodness or truth. There is no objective significance to human existence; life's meaning is only what we make it. Therefore, we have to manifest courage in a world that is not so much hostile as indifferent, and this is what the superman will do. This is dialectical courage—courage in the face of the universe's indifference. Nietzsche was saying, in essence: "Life is meaningless; therefore, have courage. Your courage is meaningless, but have it anyway."

"ANOTHER HELPER"

What do Kierkegaard and Nietzsche have to do with the work of the Holy Spirit? In the upper room on the night before His crucifixion, Jesus gave His disciples some important promises regarding the Spirit. He told them that He was about to depart and that they could not go with Him, but He promised, "I will ask the Father, and he will give you another Helper, to be with you forever" (John 14:16).

Some translations use the word "Comforter" instead of "Helper." The Greek word that is translated as "Helper" or "Comforter" is *parakletos*; it is the source of the English word *paraclete*. This word includes a prefix, *para-*, that means "alongside," and a root that is a form of the verb *kletos*, which means "to call." So, a *parakletos* was someone who was called to stand alongside another. It usually was applied to an attorney, but not just any attorney. Technically, the *parakletos* was the family attorney who was on a permanent retainer. Any time a problem arose in the family, the *parakletos* was on call, and he would come immediately to assist in the struggle. That is the way it is in our relationship with the Holy Spirit. We are part of the family of God, and the family attorney is the Holy Spirit Himself. He is always present to come alongside us and help in times of troubles.

I believe that most New Testament translations in English do a poor job of translating *parakletos*, particularly those that render it as "comforter." That translation misses the point. When Jesus said He would ask the Father to send the disciples another Paraclete, He was not talking about Someone who would come and heal their wounds when they were bruised and broken. Of course, one of the vital works of the Holy Spirit is to bring consolation to broken hearts; He is a balm in Gilead when we are in the midst of grief and mourning. But we must remember the context in which Jesus promised to send the Spirit—He was telling His disciples that He was about to leave them. They were going to be without Him in the midst of a hostile world, where they would be hated as He had been hated. Every moment of their lives would be filled with pressure, hostility, and persecution from the world. No one wants to enter that kind of scenario without help.

The translators of the King James Version chose to render *parakletos* with the English word "Comforter" because at that time the English language was more closely connected to its historical roots in Latin. Today, we understand the word *comfort* to mean ease and solace in the midst of trouble. But its original meaning was different. It is derived from the Latin word *comfortis*, which consisted of a prefix (*com-*, meaning "with) and a root (*fortis*, meaning "strong"). So, originally the word carried the meaning "with strength." Therefore, the King James Version translators were telling us that the Holy Spirit comes to the people of Christ not to heal their wounds *after* a battle but to strengthen them *before* and *during* a struggle. The idea is that the church operates not so much as a hospital but as an army, and the

Holy Spirit comes to empower and strengthen Christians, to ensure victory or conquest.

"MORE THAN CONQUERORS"

So, Nietzsche said, "Life is meaningless, but have courage anyway." Jesus also called His people to be courageous in the face of difficulty, adversity, and hostility, but He did not call them to a groundless courage. As we know, Jesus told His disciples, "Take heart" (John 16:33), or, as some translations put it, "Be of good cheer." However, He did not simply tell them to take heart for the sake of taking heart. He gave them a reason why they ought to have a sense of confidence and assurance for the Christian life. He said, "Take heart; I have overcome the world."

Nietzsche wanted a superman, a conqueror. He should have looked to Christ. He overcame the world, and He did it in the power of the same Spirit that He sends to His people. The Holy Spirit comes to give strength and power to the people of God. As a result, the Scriptures say, "We are more than conquerors through him who loved us" (Rom. 8:37). That is a step above Nietzsche.

So, the work of the Holy Spirit supplements the work

of Christ. Christ was the first Paraclete, who came to strengthen us by His atoning death. Now, the empowerment to live the life that Christ has called us to live comes to us by the Holy Spirit.

Chapter Four

THE SANCTIFIER

Have you ever wondered why the Holy Spirit is called "the Holy Spirit"? He is holy, of course, but God the Father is also known for His unblemished holiness, and that holiness is an attribute also of God the Son. There is no sense in which the Holy Spirit possesses a greater degree or measure of holiness than the other two members of the Trinity. So, it is not His superabundant holiness that leads us to call Him the Holy Spirit. Likewise, the Spirit is indeed a spirit, but God the Father is also a spirit, and God the Son is a spirit in His being, as the *Logos*, the second person of the Trinity. Thus, it is clearly not because He is a spirit that we designate the third person of the Trinity as the Holy Spirit.

There are a couple of reasons why the third person is known as the Holy Spirit. First, the term *holy* is attached to His title because of the particular task the Spirit performs in our redemption. Among the persons of the Trinity, the Spirit is the principal actor who works for our sanctification, enabling the process by which we are conformed to the image of Christ and made holy.

Christians often ask me, "What's the will of God for my life?" They have all kinds of questions about who they should marry, what career they should pursue, and myriad other decisions. But the Bible is very clear about the principal will of God for our lives. The Apostle Paul writes, "This is the will of God, your sanctification" (1 Thess. 4:3a). At other times, I hear Christians speak of being led by the Spirit to do something. Yes, the Holy Spirit at times leads people to specific destinations or to specific tasks, but the primary leading of the Spirit, as set forth in Scripture, is to holiness. It is His power working in us that helps us grow in holiness. We need to be very careful to go to the pages of the Scripture to learn about God's will and the leading of the Spirit, and not simply to listen to the popular teachings of the Christian subculture in which we live. So, a primary reason why the Holy Spirit is called the Holy Spirit is because it is His specific task to enable followers of Christ in their quest for sanctification.

Second, the third person is called the Holy Spirit because there is more then one kind of spirit. The Scriptures make a distinction between the spirit of man and the Spirit of God. But even more important for our consideration here, the Bible speaks about evil spirits, spirits who are not from God, demonic spirits that desire to impede the progress of the Christian in his quest for sanctification. The key difference between these evil spirits and the Holy Spirit is precisely at the point of holiness. Evil spirits are unholy, but the Holy Spirit is holy altogether. It is because of this distinction that the Apostle John warns us, "Do not believe every spirit, but test the spirits to see whether they are from God" (1 John 4:1a).

JUSTIFYING OUR SIN

I emphasize these points for this reason: In the Christian world, many of us are masters at justifying our sin, and one of the chief ways we do it is by saying we were led to do such and such by the Holy Spirit. This is not a problem that I encounter once every ten years. At least once a week I talk to a professing Christian who tells me he or she is getting a divorce without biblical grounds, entering into a marriage in opposition to the biblical qualification for marriage, or running a business according to unscriptural principles. They are doing this and that, and without fail they tell me they feel free to do it because "I prayed about it and God has given me peace" or "The Holy Spirit has led me to do this."

When I hear these kinds of justifications for unbiblical behavior, I realize the people may actually believe what they are telling me, but they are not speaking the truth. They are speaking in error—very serious error. I know this for two reasons, and these reasons are grounded in two crucial designations about the character of the Spirit of God. The first is that He is the *Holy* Spirit. The second is that Jesus repeatedly called Him "the Spirit of truth" (John 14:17; 15:26; 16:13). The Holy Spirit never entices us to do something that is unholy. Neither does the Holy Spirit ever incline us to embrace a lie.

We refer to the Bible as the Word of God, and so it is. One of the reasons why the church has confessed its faith that the Scriptures are the Word of God is the biblical claim that the words of sacred Scripture were originally inspired by God the Holy Spirit. Of course, the Bible teaches that the Holy Spirit not only inspired the writing of the biblical books, He works to illumine the Scriptures and to apply them to our understanding. Paul writes, "God is not a God of confusion" (1 Cor. 14:33a), and that includes the Holy Spirit. This means that the Holy Spirit never teaches us to do something that He explicitly forbids in sacred Scripture.

So, when the Bible says we are to test the spirits to see if they are from God, how are we to do it? What kind of a test should we employ? Obviously the test must be a biblical test, because we know that in the Scriptures we have the teaching of the Spirit of truth. Therefore, if I have an internal inclination, a hunch, or a desire, and I want to associate that internal leading with the Holy Spirit, but I also see that this inclination in my heart is clearly opposed to what is taught in Scripture, I have proof positive that I am confusing lust, covetousness, or some other internal feeling with the leading of the Holy Spirit. That is a ghastly thing to do.

We almost never hear about this in the Christian community these days, because Christians easily make themselves seem spiritual by saying that God laid this or that on their hearts or God led them to do various things. Every time I hear such a claim, I want to say to the person: "How do you *know* God laid that on your heart? How do you know that's not a manifestation of your own ambition or your own avarice?" I want the person to show me the biblical basis for his claim. As I said above, I do not doubt that the Holy Spirit can put a burden on a believer and can lead a believer supernaturally, but He always does this within and through the Scriptures. He never goes against His own revelation in the Bible. So, the way to test the spirits is to judge them by the Spirit's own truth.

HOSTILITY TO DOCTRINE

Part of our growth in sanctification is growth in our understanding of the things of God. Unfortunately, I have grave concerns about a movement that seems to be sweeping through the Christian world. I find that there is a pervasive indifference and sometimes hostility to the study of doctrine or theology. I have actually heard it said that there are two kinds of people in the church, people who think theology is important and people who do not think it is important. But there was a corollary comment—it was said that people who care about theology are not loving, and that is a problem because God is more concerned that we be loving than that we know theology.

I was deeply distressed when I heard that. Of course, I had heard expressions of antipathy to doctrine before, and I grant that the study of doctrine can lead to a dead orthodoxy that is not godly at all. I think we all know that it is possible to study doctrine as an intellectual exercise and have no love for God or for other people. But it is another matter to generalize this problem and conclude that if we do pursue the study of Christian theology, we absolutely cannot be loving, so the best way to be loving is to avoid theology. Think of the implications of that. Such a conclusion means that the best way to be loving is to avoid as much as we possibly can an understanding of the things of God. The study of theology is simply the study of the character of God, whose crowning virtue is love. Sound theology actually teaches the central importance of love and inclines us to love the God of the Scriptures and other people as well.

Such antipathy to doctrine usually is expressed in the context of a theological controversy. People can get nasty on both sides of theological controversies. But others shy away from all controversy. They often say, "I don't care about this controversy or about doctrine in general, I just think we need to be more loving toward one another." But is it loving to allow serious theological error to continue unchallenged? Was Paul unloving when he disputed daily in the marketplace about the things of God (Acts 17:17)? Was Jesus unloving when He contradicted the teaching of the Pharisees? Were the prophets of ancient Israel unloving when they rebuked and admonished the false prophets? Was Elijah unloving when he disputed with the prophets of Baal (1 Kings 18)? I cannot imagine someone in the crowd on Mount Carmel that day saying: "You people can follow Elijah if you want to, but I'm not going to. He may have truth on his side, but he is not loving. Look what he did to these prophets of Baal. How unloving!" Contending for the truth of God is an act of love, not a sign of an absence of love. If we love God, if we love Christ, if we love the church, we must love the truth that defines the very essence of Christianity.

I once heard another disturbing comment: "Christianity is about relationships, not about propositions." The person went on to say that Christianity is also concerned about truth, but I could not quite put those two statements together. If the Christian faith is not about propositions, what kind of truth is it about? I believe the influence of existentialism in the culture in general and in the church in particular has produced something that was unknown in previous generations: relational theology. Simply put, relational theology is a theological system that has content and meaning determined by relationships. It is only a half step removed from pure relativism. This is the kind of theology that says if you believe that God is one and I believe that God is three in one, what really matters is our personal relationship. Truth is determined by the relationships, not by the propositions. For example, if I say Jesus died on the cross as an atonement and someone else says His death was not an atonement, we do not discuss it lest we sever our relationship. The relationship must be preserved even if the truth is lost.

THE GOAL OF KNOWING GOD

Emil Brunner, the twentieth-century Swiss theologian and one of the fathers of neoorthodox theology, wrote a little book titled *Truth as Encounter*. His thesis was that when we study the things of God, we are not studying truth in the abstract. We want to understand theology not merely so that we can make an A on a theology exam. We want to understand the doctrine of God so that we can understand God, so that we can meet the living God in His Word and deepen our personal relationship with Him. But we cannot deepen a relationship with someone if we do not know anything about him. So, the propositions of Scripture are not an end in themselves but a means to an end. However, they are a *necessary* means to the end. Thus, to say Christianity is not about propositions but about relationships is to establish an extremely dangerous false dichotomy. It is to insult the Spirit of truth, whose propositions they are. These propositions should be our very meat and drink, for they define the Christian life.

Recently I read some letters to the editor of a Christian magazine. One of them disparaged Christian scholars with advanced degrees. The letter writer charged that such men would enjoy digging into word studies of Christ's teachings in the ancient languages in order to demonstrate that He did not really say what He seems to say in our English Bibles. Obviously there was a negative attitude toward any serious study of the Word of God. Of course, there are scholars who are like this, who study a word in six different languages and still end up missing its meaning, but that does not mean we must not engage in any serious study of the Word of God lest we end up like these ungodly scholars. Another letter writer expressed the view that people who engage in the study of doctrine are not concerned about the pain people experience in this world. In my experience, however, it is virtually impossible to experience pain and not ask questions about truth. We all want to know the truth about suffering, and specifically, where is God in our pain. That is a theological concern. The answer comes to us from the Scriptures, which reveal the mind of God Himself through the agency of the Holy Spirit, who is called the Spirit of truth. We cannot love God at all if we do not love His truth.

It is very sad to me that in today's sophisticated Western culture, people are more familiar with the twelve signs of the Zodiac than with the twelve tribes of Israel or the twelve Apostles. Our world likes to see itself as sophisticated and technological, but it remains filled with superstition. Christians are not immune to this. We, too, can succumb to the new-age desire for the power to manipulate our environment. We do not have to go as far as accepting the foolish idea that the courses of the stars determine our destinies, our prosperity, our achievements, and our successes. However, it is equally superstitious to equate our feelings and inclinations with the leading of the Holy Spirit. It seems so much more exciting to live with a freewheeling openness to the leading of the Holy Spirit rather than practicing the laborious discipline of mastering His Word. This is exceedingly dangerous ground. If we want to do the will of the Father, we need to study the Word of the Father—and leave the magic to the astrologers.

Chapter Five

THE ANOINTER

Throughout the Old Testament, the Holy Spirit is a fleeting presence. He appears from time to time, but His ministry is never described in great detail. The one role He plays repeatedly is that of empowering leaders of Israel for their God-given tasks. These leaders were those who were given the "anointed" tasks of prophet, priest, and king. The Spirit rested on these men, though His presence with them was usually temporary; He anointed them to empower them for specific tasks.

There are numerous Old Testament examples of the

Spirit anointing leaders: "The Spirit of the LORD was upon [Othniel], and he judged Israel" (Judg. 3:10); "Then the Spirit of the Lord was upon Jephthah" (11:29a); "And the Spirit of God rushed upon Saul" (1 Sam. 11:6a); "Then Samuel took the horn of oil and anointed him in the midst of his brothers. And the Spirit of the Lord rushed upon David from that day forward" (16:13a). Similarly, we see examples of the Spirit resting upon the prophets when they received their call to speak for God (1 Kings 17:2; Jer. 1:4). And the Spirit's anointing of the priests is portrayed by their anointing in oil (Ex. 29:21). Again, however, these examples show that the Spirit's anointing for ministry was limited. But the Old Testament gave hints that the nature of the Spirit's anointing would be much broader and lasting someday.

One of these hints is found in the book of Numbers. We read there:

Now the rabble that was among them had a strong craving. And the people of Israel also wept again and said, "Oh that we had meat to eat! We remember the fish we ate in Egypt that cost nothing, the cucumbers, the melons, the leeks, the onions, and the garlic. But now our strength is dried up, and there is nothing at all but this manna to look at." Now the manna was like coriander seed, and its appearance like that of bdellium. The people went about and gathered it and ground it in handmills or beat it in mortars and boiled it in pots and made cakes of it. And the taste of it was like the taste of cakes baked with oil. When the dew fell upon the camp in the night, the manna fell with it. (11:4–9)

Let me set the scene here. God redeemed Israel from bondage in Egypt. As He led them through the desert toward the Promised Land, He cared for their daily needs, giving them miraculous provisions from heaven in the form of manna. At first, the people of Israel rejoiced in their freedom and the kind hand of providence that gave them food to eat every day. But soon they became dissatisfied. They forgot the whips, the torture, the sweat, and the impoverishment of their slavery; now their deepest dreams were filled with visions of the fish, the cucumbers, the melons, the leeks, the onions, and the garlic they had eaten in Egypt. They were unhappy about having to eat the same thing, manna, for every meal. When I read about their dissatisfaction, I cannot help but chuckle. The grass really is always greener on the other side, or so we assume.

As the account in Numbers continues, we read, "Moses heard the people weeping throughout their clans, everyone at the door of his tent. And the anger of the LORD blazed hotly, and Moses was displeased" (v. 10). It seems everyone was displeased at this point. In Moses' case, however, it was much more. He was beside himself:

Moses said to the LORD, "Why have you dealt ill with your servant? And why have I not found favor in your sight, that you lay the burden of all this people on me? Did I conceive all this people? Did I give them birth, that you should say to me, 'Carry them in your bosom, as a nurse carries a nursing child,' to the land that you swore to give their fathers? Where am I to get meat to give to all this people? For they weep before me and say, 'Give us meat, that we may eat.' I am not able to carry all this people alone; the burden is too heavy for me. If you will treat me like this, kill me at once, if I find favor in your sight, that I may not see my wretchedness." (vv. 11–15)

We can judge the depths of Moses' despair by the words of the desperate prayer he made on this occasion: "God, if You like me at all, if You care about me at all, kill me right now, because I can't take this anymore." He had thousands of people screaming at him to give them something he had no way to provide. At that point, death seemed preferable to continuing to lead the Israelites.

God's response was not what Moses expected:

Then the LORD said to Moses, "Gather for me seventy men of the elders of Israel, whom you know to be the elders of the people and officers over them, and bring them to the tent of meeting, and let them take their stand there with you. And I will come down and talk with you there. And I will take some of the Spirit that is on you and put it on them, and they shall bear the burden of the people with you, so that you may not bear it yourself alone. And say to the people, 'Consecrate yourselves for tomorrow, and you shall eat meat, for you have wept in the hearing of the LORD, saying, "Who will give us meat to eat? For it was better for us in Egypt." Therefore the LORD will give you meat, and you shall eat. You shall not eat just one day, or two days, or five days, or ten days, or twenty days, but a whole month, until it comes out at your nostrils and becomes loathsome to you, because you have rejected the LORD who is among you and have wept before him, saying, "Why did we come out of Egypt?"'" (vv. 16–20)

I think that the lesson here is this: Be careful what you pray for. The people were crying for meat, so God said: "OK, if you want meat, I'll give you meat. I'll give you meat for breakfast, meat for lunch, meat for dinner, and meat for a midnight snack, and not just for one or two days but for a whole month, until it is coming out of your noses." God said He would give them meat until they could not stand the sight of it anymore.

It would seem that Moses should have been relieved at this news. God was going to give the people what they wanted, taking the pressure off Moses. It would have been logical for Moses to say: "Thank you, Lord, for taking charge of this situation. I appreciate it very much." But this is not what happened. Instead, Moses had a crisis of faith. He said to God: "The people among whom I am number six hundred thousand on foot, and you have said, 'I will give them meat, that they may eat a whole month!' Shall flocks and herds be slaughtered for them, and be enough for them? Or shall all the fish of the sea be gathered together for them, and be enough for them?" (vv. 21–22).

When Moses spoke of six hundred thousand men of foot, he was referring to the size of the Israelites army, the men who were ready for battle. This figure did not include the young boys, the children, the elderly, the infirm, or the women. He probably was responsible for well over 2 million people. Moses could not see any way that God could fulfill His promises to give this vast host of people meat to eat for a month.

I love God's response: "And the LORD said to Moses, 'Is the LORD's hand shortened? Now you shall see whether my word will come true for you or not'" (v. 23). Basically, God asked Moses, "Am I God or am I not God?" Then He challenged Moses to simply watch and see what He would do.

Hearing that, Moses said no more. He simply did as God had commanded him: "Moses went out and told the people the words of the LORD. And he gathered seventy men of the elders of the people and placed them around the tent. Then the LORD came down in the cloud and spoke to him, and took some of the Spirit that was on him and put it on the seventy elders. And as soon as the Spirit rested on them, they prophesied. But they did not continue doing it" (vv. 24–25).

ASSISTANTS FOR MOSES

As we begin to explore this important incident, it is helpful to consider an earlier event that is recorded in Exodus 18. We are told that after God brought the people of Israel out of Egypt, Moses' father-in-law, Jethro, the priest of Midian, came to visit him at the Israelite camp at Sinai. During his visit, Jethro saw that Moses sat to decide disputes among the people from morning till evening (vv. 1–13). Then we read:

> When Moses' father-in-law saw all that he was doing for the people, he said, "What is this that you are doing for the people? Why do you sit alone, and all the people stand around you from morning till evening?" And Moses said to his father-in-law, "Because the people come to me to inquire of God; when they have a dispute, they come to me and I decide between one person and another, and I make them know the statutes of God and his laws." Moses' father-in-law said to him, "What you are doing is

not good. You and the people with you will certainly wear yourselves out, for the thing is too heavy for you. You are not able to do it alone. Now obey my voice; I will give you advice, and God be with you! You shall represent the people before God and bring their cases to God, and you shall warn them about the statutes and the laws, and make them know the way in which they must walk and what they must do. Moreover, look for able men from all the people, men who fear God, who are trustworthy and hate a bribe, and place such men over the people as chiefs of thousands, of hundreds, of fifties, and of tens. And let them judge the people at all times. Every great matter they shall bring to you, but any small matter they shall decide themselves. So it will be easier for you, and they will bear the burden with you. If you do this, God will direct you, you will be able to endure, and all this people also will go to their place in peace." So Moses listened to the voice of his father-in-law and did all that he had said. Moses chose able men out of all Israel and made them heads over the people, chiefs of thousands, of hundreds, of fifties, and of tens. And they judged the people at all times. Any hard case they brought to Moses, but any small matter they decided themselves. (vv. 14–26)

Moses took Jethro's advice and appointed men to serve as judges under him, while he functioned as the "chief justice," hearing the most difficult cases.

In the account in Numbers, God did something similar. God had told Moses to gather seventy men who were elders of the people and to bring them to the tabernacle (11:16). God was saying: "I will ease the burden of leadership on you. I am going to give you not just one assistant but seventy." When they gathered, God took some of the Spirit that was on Moses and placed it on the seventy elders. As a result, there was no longer just one anointed leader in the camp, there were seventy-one of them.

Moses had been anointed by the Holy Spirit to act as the mediator of the old covenant. Now, God anointed seventy more people to participate in this work. It is significant that He did not give them an anointing of their own; rather, He disbursed the Spirit that was upon Moses among the seventy elders. When He did so, they all began to prophesy in a unique way, a way they had never done before and never did afterward. This outward manifestation showed that they had been empowered by the Holy Spirit.

Almost as a footnote, we then read: "Now two men remained in the camp, one named Eldad, and the other named Medad, and the Spirit rested on them. They were among those registered, but they had not gone out to the tent, and so they prophesied in the camp. And a young man ran and told Moses, 'Eldad and Medad are prophesying in the camp'" (vv. 26–27). This was scandalous. The people did not yet know that God had commanded this distribution of the Holy Spirit beyond the person of Moses to the seventy elders. When they observed Eldad and Medad prophesying, they were horrified that this might be the sign of a false prophet. So, they ran to inform Moses about it.

When the news reached Moses, his assistant, Joshua, was particularly upset: "And Joshua the son of Nun, the assistant of Moses from his youth, said, 'My lord Moses, stop them'" (v. 28). Why did Joshua make this request? Was he opposed to prophecy? Was he against the power of the Holy Spirit? No, Joshua was simply concerned that this was a threat to Moses' leadership. He saw it as an attempted uprising against the duly constituted authority of the Old Testament church.

Moses' response is vital for our understanding of the work of the Holy Spirit. We read: "But Moses said to him, 'Are you jealous for my sake? Would that all the LORD's people were prophets, that the LORD would put his Spirit on them!'" (v. 29). Whereas Joshua protested the expansion of the anointing of the Holy Spirit to empower God's people for ministry, Moses delighted in it. He even expressed the desire that God would place His Spirit on each and every one of His people.

In ancient Israel, during the time of Moses, this idea that the Spirit might rest on every believer was merely a hope or a prayer on the lips of Moses. Later, however, that hope became a prophecy. The prophet Joel wrote: "And it shall come to pass afterward, that I will pour out my Spirit on all flesh; your sons and your daughters shall prophesy, your old men shall dream dreams, and your young men shall see visions. Even on the male and female servants in those days I will pour out my Spirit" (2:28–29). Under the Spirit's inspiration, Joel said that in the last days, God would pour out His Spirit on "all flesh," that is, on all the people of God. The empowering of the Holy Spirit for ministry would not be limited to isolated individuals or to a small core of people, but every person in the fellowship of God would be so endowed.

PRAYER AND PROPHECY FULFILLED

What was a prayer for Moses and a prophecy for Joel became a historical reality on the day of Pentecost, when God took of the Spirit that was upon Jesus, the Mediator of the new covenant, and distributed Him not to seventy but to all the believers.

Jesus had told the disciples that this would happen. In the book of Acts, Luke writes: "And while staying with them [Jesus] ordered them not to depart from Jerusalem, but to wait for the promise of the Father, which, he said, 'you heard from me; for John baptized with water, but you will be baptized with the Holy Spirit not many days from now'" (1:4–5). One of the last things Jesus told His disciples before He ascended to His Father was that they should stay for a short time in Jerusalem so that they might receive the fulfillment of a promise the Father had made. He was alluding to the promise of the baptism of the Holy Spirit in the prophecy of Joel. He told them it would happen in the very near future.

Luke continues: "So when they had come together, they asked him, 'Lord, will you at this time restore the kingdom to Israel?' He said to them, 'It is not for you to know times or seasons that the Father has fixed by his own authority. But you will receive power when the Holy Spirit has come upon you, and you will be my witnesses in Jerusalem and in all Judea and Samaria, and to the end of the earth'" (vv. 6–8). Here Jesus associated the baptism of the Spirit with power to be His witnesses.

In all the passages we have discussed—Numbers 11, Joel 2, and especially here in Acts 1—the anointing of the Holy Spirit is associated with some sort of endowment, some gracious divine gifting. The Greek word for this kind of gift is *charisma*. Thus, the gifts the Spirit brings are known as the "charismatic" gifts or the *charismata*. The Spirit gives these gifts to Christ's church to empower the people of God to carry out the mission that Christ gave to His people—to bear witness to Him to the uttermost parts of the earth.

So, that was the promise. On the day of Pentecost, the Spirit indeed came upon the disciples with power:

When the day of Pentecost arrived, they were all together in one place. And suddenly there came from heaven a sound like a mighty rushing wind, and it filled the entire house where they were sitting. And divided tongues as of fire appeared to them and rested on each one of them. And they were all filled with the Holy Spirit and began to speak in other tongues as the Spirit gave them utterance. Now there were dwelling in Jerusalem Jews, devout men from every nation under heaven. And at this sound the multitude came together, and they were bewildered, because each one was hearing them speak in his own language. And they were amazed and astonished, saying, "Are not all these who are speaking Galileans? . . . We hear them telling in our own tongues the mighty works of God." (Acts 2:1–11)

Pentecost was an annual feast that was held in Jerusalem. Jewish pilgrims from all over the world came to Jerusalem for the feast of Pentecost. So, there was a huge assembly of Jews from many regions speaking many languages. But the feast was interrupted by a supernatural event that was marked by a visible manifestation of the Holy Spirit—tongues of fire that rested over the heads of the disciples—and an audible manifestation—the disciples spoke about "the mighty works of God" in the languages of all of those who were present.

After that anointing by the Spirit, the disciples were

changed men. They began to preach that Jesus was the Christ, the Savior, and they would not be silenced even by threats of execution. Soon, they began to take the message of the gospel everywhere, just as Jesus had commanded them, and soon it was said of them that they had "turned the world upside down" (Acts 17:6). Such is the power of the anointing the Spirit gives to each and every person who trusts in Jesus Christ under the new covenant.

Martin Luther, the great German Reformer of the sixteenth century, spoke of "the priesthood of all believers." Some take this to mean that there is to be no distinction in the church between clergy and laity, but that is not what Luther meant. He was saying that the work of the kingdom of God is not given solely to those who have the vocations of preacher, teacher, deacon, or elder. Rather, every Christian is called to participate in the ministry of Christ and in the ministry of the church. That can be intimidating, but with that call comes the gift of the Holy Spirit, who anoints and empowers all of Christ's people to serve Him.

Chapter Six

THE ILLUMINATOR

In the first year of my academic career, I was teaching at a college in western Pennsylvania. In the spring semester, a coed made an appointment with me to discuss a personal problem. She was quite distressed because she was experiencing what is sometimes called "senioritis." She was in her last semester of her senior year, but she was not married, she was not dating, and she had no prospects for a relationship with a man at the time. She was a devout and earnest Christian, so she wanted to know whether it would be wrong for her to pray to find a mate. I told her that there was nothing at all wrong with praying that God would provide her with a husband, and I urged her to do so.

About two weeks later, she came to see me again, and this time she was filled with joy and elation. She said, "I've been praying for two weeks that God would give me a husband, and He's answered my prayers." I said, "You have met someone?" She said: "No, I haven't met him yet. But I know I will very shortly. You see, last night I lucky dipped." Now, I had never heard of such a thing as "lucky dipping," so I asked her what she meant. She said: "Well, I was praying, and I had my Bible in front of me, and I asked God whether He was going to provide me with a husband. Then I closed my eyes, opened my Bible at random, and dropped my finger on the page. When I opened my eyes, my finger was pointing to Zechariah 9:9, which says: 'Rejoice greatly, O daughter of Zion! Shout aloud, O daughter of Jerusalem! Behold, your king is coming to you; righteous and having salvation is he, humble and mounted on a donkey, on a colt, the foal of a donkey.' That was God's answer to my prayer. The Spirit revealed to me that I am going to be married."

This was an example of "pneumatic exegesis," which is just a fancy term for lucky dipping. It has to do with interpreting the Bible through some kind of spiritual machination. It does not simply border on magic and superstition, it crosses that border. This dear college student of mine had engaged in a way of interpreting Scripture that really is an offense against God the Holy Spirit. Turning the Bible into a magic talisman is certainly not according to the intent of the Spirit in His work of inspiring the Bible.

HOW THE SPIRIT USES THE WORD

There was a similar episode in the life of Augustine, the great theologian of the first millennium. Before his conversion, Augustine earned a reputation for living a wild, unbridled, and licentious lifestyle. His godly mother, Monica, prayed earnestly for a long time that her son would come to Christ. One day, as Augustine recounts in his memoir, *Confessions*, he was meditating in a garden, trying to understand the truth amid his confusion over the various philosophical systems of his day. Some children were playing a game nearby, and Augustine could hear them chanting an odd refrain: "*Tolle lege, tolle lege*," which means, "Take up and read, take up and read." Augustine found a copy of the Christian Scriptures and began to read where the pages fell open. They fell open to the book of Romans, where Paul said: "Let us walk properly as in the daytime, not in orgies and drunkenness, not in sexual immorality and sensuality, not in quarreling and jealousy. But put on the Lord Jesus Christ, and make no provision for the flesh, to gratify its desires" (Rom. 13:13–14). When Augustine's eyes fell on that text, he was stricken with guilt and awakened to the things of God. At that moment, he was born again by the Holy Spirit.

What is the difference between Augustine's experience and the experience of my student in college? Augustine did not try to discern God's will through a magical process. He simply picked up the Scriptures and happened to read in a certain place. Most important, God did not give the text Augustine read some meaning that the Holy Spirit did not intend when He inspired Paul to write it. Rather, the Spirit enabled Augustine to understand what the text really meant. There was no magic in it.

I was converted to Christ through a discussion in a college dormitory one evening in 1957. A fellow student who was a Christian was talking to me about the things of God and quoting all kinds of things from the Bible. Most of it went right over my head and I do not remember what he said. But he began to speak about the wisdom of God, and when he did, he opened his Bible to the book of Ecclesiastes and read a few verses, including this one: "If a tree falls to the south or to the north, in the place where the tree falls, there it will lie" (11:3b). As I heard those words, suddenly I was overwhelmed by thinking about myself as a tree that had fallen and was lying inert, torpid, rotting in the woods. I saw that I was in just that spiritual condition; I was a fallen tree, and I would lie there forever unless God did something. That was not a misapplication of that text. I believe that God the Holy Spirit used that text to awaken me to saving faith.

These are examples of what we call divine illumination, yet another important work of the Holy Spirit. We must distinguish the Spirit's work of illumination from His vitally important work of revelation. The Holy Spirit inspired the biblical revelation, the truth of God that is unfolded and unveiled for us in the Bible. This is information that comes to us ultimately from the mind of God Himself. Illumination, by contrast, brings no new information. It rests upon the information the Spirit has already given in the Scriptures. When the Spirit used that childish chant to provoke Augustine to read the text of Romans, He did not at that moment give new information for Augustine's sake. Rather,

He simply directed Augustine to read a passage of Scripture that was there for everyone else to read. But thousands and thousands of people had read that text and not seen themselves in it. They had not been convicted by it but remained untouched because they remained blind to its import and power. But Augustine experienced the illumination of the Spirit. In other words, the Spirit worked in Augustine to help him understand the truth of God in the words he read.

SEARCHING "THE DEPTHS OF GOD"

Christians are to be numbered among the illuminati, those who have been enlightened—not by some guru from the Himalayas, but by the Holy Spirit employing the light of God's Word. We see this clearly in the Apostle Paul's first epistle to the Corinthians, where we read:

> Yet among the mature we do impart wisdom, although it is not a wisdom of this age or of the rulers of this age, who are doomed to pass away. But we impart a secret and hidden wisdom of God, which God decreed before the ages for our glory. None of the rulers of this age understood this, for if

they had, they would not have crucified the Lord of glory. But, as it is written, "What no eye has seen, nor ear heard, nor the heart of man imagined, what God has prepared for those who love him"—these things God has revealed to us through the Spirit. For the Spirit searches everything, even the depths of God. (2:6–10)

What does Paul mean when he says "the Spirit searches everything, even the depths of God"? When we use the word *search*, we usually are referring to the act of trying to find something that we want to locate or discover. If I am on a quest for knowledge, a search for knowledge, I am trying to learn something I do not presently know. So, when Paul says the Spirit searches the depths of God, he seems to be implying that the third person of the Trinity is pursuing some knowledge that He lacks. But if we conclude that there are certain things the Holy Spirit does not know and needs to learn, our doctrine of the Trinity is destroyed. Such a lack of knowledge in the Spirit would deny His deity as a member of the Godhead. So, we must come at the question from the other direction, accepting what the rest of Scripture teaches about the Spirit—that He is a part of the Godhead and therefore omniscient. Thus, He does not search the depths of God to increase His own knowledge.

On the contrary, Paul is telling us here that the Holy Spirit searches the depths of God for us. The Spirit acts as a searchlight and shines on the text of Scripture when we read it, giving us the capacity to understand the meaning of it. When this happens, we see the truth of God intensely and sharply. Every one of us who is a Christian has had this experience sometime in his or her life. We are reading from the Scriptures, and suddenly a particular truth seems to jump off the page and pierce our souls. That is the work of the Holy Spirit in illumination.

In the year 1734, a sermon was preached at Northampton, Massachusetts, which I believe was one of the most important sermons ever preached on what is now U.S. soil. The man who preached it, Jonathan Edwards, is more famous for a different sermon, "Sinners in the Hands of an Angry God," which he preached in Enfield, Connecticut, in 1741. Many anthologies of American literature include "Sinners in the Hands of an Angry God" as a representative example of writing in Colonial New England. But the earlier sermon that I believe was so very important was given this title: "A Divine and Supernatural Light, Immediately Imparted to the Soul by the Spirit of God, Shown to Be Both Scriptural and Rational Doctrine." This sermon is not very well known or widely circulated, but I think that if any sermon captures Edwards' genius, it is this one. In this sermon, Edwards was speaking about supernatural illumination.

Edwards defines this spiritual light by saying:

And it may be thus described: a true sense of the divine excellency of the things revealed in the word of God, and a conviction of the truth and reality of them thence arising. This spiritual light primarily consists in the former of these, *viz.*, a real sense and apprehension of the divine excellency of things revealed in the word of God. A spiritual and saving conviction of the truth and reality of these things, arises from such a sight of their divine excellency and glory; so that this conviction of their truth is an effect and natural consequence of this sight of their divine glory.[1]

---

1 Jonathan Edwards, "A Divine and Supernatural Light, Immediately Imparted to the Soul by the Spirit of God, Shown to be Both Scriptural and Rational Doctrine," http://www.ccel.org/e/edwards/sermons/supernatural_light.html, accessed July 5, 2012.

According to Edwards, the primary effect of the Spirit's work of illumination is to awaken in us a sense of the divine excellence of the things of God. We may be persuaded that Christ is divine and still not grasp the sweetness of that idea. There may not yet be affection for Him in our hearts or souls. The Spirit awakens in us a sensibility to the excellence of the things of God. But He does not operate against the Word of God. The Spirit works in the Word, with the Word, and through the Word. In other words, He takes us to the revelation of God and shows it to us in such a way that He overcomes our natural hostility or bias against the truth of God and shows us the loveliness of it. Just as Ezekiel swallowed the scroll with its bitter words and found them suddenly sweet as honey in his mouth (3:3), so the words of God become sweet to all who view them under the searchlight of the Spirit.

About the Author

Dr. R. C. Sproul is the founder and chairman of Ligonier Ministries, an international multimedia ministry based in Sanford, Florida. He also serves as senior minister of preaching and teaching at Saint Andrew's, a Reformed congregation in Sanford, and as president of Reformation Bible College, and his teaching can be heard around the world on the daily radio program *Renewing Your Mind*.

During his distinguished academic career, Dr. Sproul helped train men for the ministry as a professor at several theological seminaries.

He is the author of more than eighty books, including *The Holiness of God, Chosen by God, The Invisible Hand, Faith Alone, A Taste of Heaven, Truths We Confess, The Truth of the Cross*, and *The Prayer of the Lord*. He also served as general editor of *The Reformation Study Bible* and has written several children's books, including *The Prince's Poison Cup*.

Dr. Sproul and his wife, Vesta, make their home in Longwood, Florida.